ALLIGATOR SNAPS

A TONGUE-TWISTER'S
ALPHABET OF MANY
MEANIE BEASTIES
AND OTHER POEMS

To Finley with best wishes from Dennis Carter 21.10.14

by DENNIS CARTER

Illustrated by Dunstan Carter

catchfire publications

September 2014

Pentre Farm, Woodhill, Oswestry,
Shropshire. SY10 9AS

email:
dennisbcarter@hotmail.com

blog:
denniscarterpoetry.wordpress.com

All rights with the author

ISBN 978-0-9533499-6-8

Notes:
1. **Tongue-twisters:** can you say the 26 animal poems very quickly WITHOUT making mistakes?
2. **Zephyrosaurus** was a small dinosaur that lived in the mountains and could run very fast. Its name is made from Zephyr, Greek for wind.
3. **Evacuation Stories** (pages 14-15) are based on real people's experiences of evacuation.
4. **An Ode** (pages 20-21) is a very old kind of poem which praises something.
5. **Olive** (pages 31 & 36) is the author's two year old granddaughter.
6. **Allan** (page 31) is the author's uncle and his mother's brother.
7. **Winnie** (pages 32-34) is the author's mother when she was a little girl in the 1930s.

Thanks to: The teachers and children in schools in Anglesey, Cheshire, Conwy, Denbighshire, Gwynedd, Lincolnshire, Powys, West Yorkshire and Wrexham who have listened to these poems.

A TONGUE TWISTER'S ALPHABET OF MANY MEANIE BEASTIES

A a
ALLIGATOR
alligator

Alligator snaps at
sprats in the water.
Alligator smacks
a fat tail on the bank.
Alligator snapped
and alligator smacked
and into the river sank.

B b
BATS
bats

Bats bother bellringers
by being in belfries
and by bobbing bottoms up
like brown lightbulbs.
By billowing about bells
bats become a big, big
bother to bellringers.

C c
COCKROACHES
cockroaches

Caution! Take care!
Under the cloak of night
cockroaches crawl
from cracks in unclean
creaky floors and damp
carpets in clutters,
causing crappy smells
then craftily creep
through kitchen doors
into crannies behind
cupboards and cookers
to crunch crusts,
crumbs and crud.

D d
DOGS
dogs

Dirty dogs don't care.
Down drives and in our
doorways , even among
the dainty daisies,
dirty dogs devilishly
dodge, dash and dare
to do their dirty doings.

E e
EARWIGS
earwigs

'Ere come the earwigs,
so evil everyone of 'em.
I've 'eard they enter your
earholes and even
eat out your eyeballs.
Eeeeeeeeeeeeeee!
'Ere come the earwigs so
'elp yourself to earplugs
or earmuffs or 'elmets.

F f
FLEA
flea

Flea fleck, flippy fleck,
flitting in a flip flop.
Flip, flit, flit nip,
feeding on a fat hip,
flicky, flecky, flipping
flea itch, itch, itch.

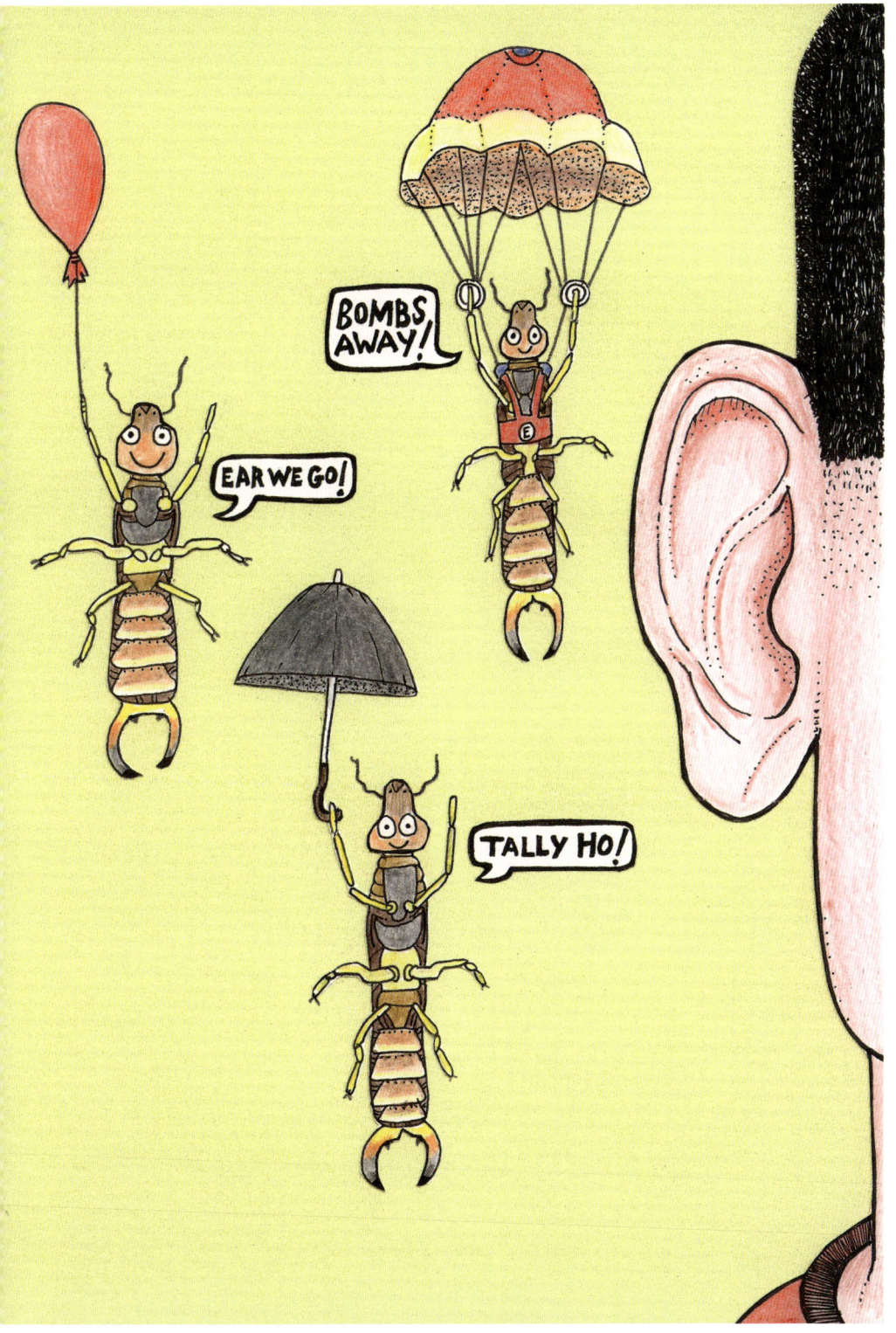

G g
GORILLAS
gorillas

Gorillas are the greatest
gropers and grabbers.
On grassy ground in
groveling groups they gripe
and grumble then go off
gripping on groovy grapevines
and grin gormlessly,
the goggle-eyed grapplers.

H h
HYENA
hyena

Ha-ha-ha-ha-hyena
has this hilarious habit
of hollering his hello.
Maybe you have heard him
hawing with no harmony
or seen him hacking at
dead animals hectically
on hot horizons.

I i
IGUANA
iguana

Iggledy-piggledy
iguana, inside its mouth
an icky, sticky tongue
for insect catching.
All idle illusions and
italic patterns that
imitate interesting
colours in the trees.

J j
JELLYFISH
jellyfish

J-j-j-jellyfish, jellyfish,
juggling your jungle
of jolly jellylegs,
jogging and jabbling
on sea jaunts or just
jaded like old jalopies
on the juicy seashore.

K k
KOOKABURRA
kookaburra

Kookaburra, kookaburra
might have been clonked
on the head, kos he keeps
kooking up quirky songs
as if he thinks he's king
of the krooners, Mr Kool.
He kips near koala bears and
keeps the kangaroos skippy.

L l
LOCUSTS
locusts

Locusts love
to lunch on
long level lands,
leaving no life left,
not a little litter,
nor a line of corn
no lush leaf nor
leathery stem,
then lift from loam
when all is lost.

M m
MIDGES
midges

Mmmmmidges!
must they meet me
every moment
and mither me
and make me make
mistakes and muddle
me up till I am
most miserable?

N n
NEWTS
newts

Good news!
Newts need nothing
more than a nice
natural pond nearby,
neat weeds underneath
and another newt each
but no nest to make
a new lot of newts.

**O o
OCTOPUS
octopus**

Octopus has oodles
of oozing oily legs,
one on top of another
and when he opens each
leggy oar he orbits
over the ocean floor.

**P p
PIGS
pigs**

Pooh!
Pigs patter on
trotting paws and
play plodding games
in puddles.
Pooh!
The pong of playful
pigs and piglets,
plugging pink
snouts in pigswill,
plonking plump
bums to piddle
in mud porridge.
Pooh!

Q q
QUEEN BEE
queen bee

Queen Bee you
lead a quiet life,
with no quibbles
and quite a quantity
of drones queueing
up and asking no
questions and never
quarrelling then quickly
you lay squillions of
eggs of high quality,
a full quota lying like
a quilt in your nest.

**R r
RATS
rats**

Rats, rats, repulsive
running, racing rats,
a rushing riff-raff
rummaging in rotten
rubbish or rioting
like a ragamuffin rabble
on the rampage.

**S s
SLUGS
slugs**

Slithery, slathery
slugs, slowly, slyly
slide. Slimy, grimy,
slippery, slobbery,
sluggardly, slovenly
sick-making slugs.

**Tt
TOADS
toads**

Toads tread
toe to toe
into the tangled
twigs of the tired
old, torn down
tree trunks
and lie like tiny
lumps of tripe
that trump.

**U u
URCHIN
Urchin**

Under the ocean's
umbrella, undisturbed
and unassuming,
uttering no sounds
sea urchin usually
undulates up and down,
up and down,
up and down,
up...................

**V v
VIPER
viper**

Viper has very vicious vangs
and a very voracious gape.
Verily I say unto you:
avoid the viper
who'll invite you
then bite you
then vanish like
a vapour.

**W w
WOODWORMS
woodworms**

Warning: woodworms
will, without worrying,
worm their wicked
ways through all your
wonderful woodwork.
So, watch your wardrobe
wobble as the worms
(now flies) whisk away
on weirdy wings.

X x
X
x

X is not a kiss
nor a wrong sum,
neither the X-box
nor the X-files.
X is not even Xmas,
No, no, no.
X marks the criss-
cross of a spider's
web on the unused
xylophone in Xanadu.

**Y y
YAK
yak**

Yak with a mucky yuck
of hair on his yump
or yellow hump
and a wooden yoke
on his neck for yanking
ploughs years and years
ago and yearning for
breakfast, yet yawning in
the yard every morning.

**Z z
ZEPHYROSAURUS
zephyrosaurus**

Zillions of years ago
Zephyrosauruses
zoomed in mountain
zones, guzzling plants
and running crazy
in zany zigzags.
These zesty lizards
lost their zip
in the ice age.
Now they're zilch,
zero in zoos.

WW2 EVACUATION STORIES

1. Mavis in Caerleon

Rucksack on my back, gasmask on my front
I came to Caerleon afraid and hungry.
I was only five and shivered scared in
the school playground. A teacher came, she
held my hand and took me to Mrs Hughes,
soon to be my Aunty Alice and her
dad was my new Taid, who tested my sums,
set hard spellings and made me a skipping
rope with colourful handles carved from wood.
But best of all were the tall tales he told
of the days when Queen Victoria ruled.
Happy was I in my funny new home
with baths in a tub in front of the fire,
toilet in a shed down in the garden.
Huge spider shadows on the walls at night
made me shudder but I always said my
prayers like a good girl then jumped into
my huge feather bed. I went to church on
Sundays and played in the fields, gathered nuts,
scrumped fruit and picked blackberries in the lane.
When I returned to London everyone
thought I sounded like a real Taffy girl.
So I said "Bore da," and "Iechyd da"
       and "Diolch yn fawr iawn"
              when they gave me sweets.

2. Sammy in Devon

Eight year old Sammy was sent to Devon
escaping the Blitz, that great lightning fire.
Short straw Sammy might have been his nickname
when the billeting man took him to the porch
of a huge posh house, where a boy-hating
lady sent a snooty servant to the door.
One look at Sammy made her nose turn up,
"a scruffy urchin from the East End slums
of London", she thought and said to Sammy,
"No thank you. Go home!" Face so stern, up spoke
the billeting man, "But there's a war on
Ma'am, you have no choice," he said and left sad
Sammy standing there, alone and confused.
Locked in his bedroom with no toys or games
Sammy discovered the shiny wood floor,
and skated in his socks to his heart's delight.
Sammy never had a warm, cooked meal, just
a sandwich or a snack. Neither did he like
the stony school with very strict teachers,
harsh rules and sticks. So Sammy pinched paper,
Sammy robbed a stamp and wrote home to Mum.
On the next train over she came and said
 "You'll not stay here a minute more" to Sammy
and to the maid "Tell that to Lady Cruelty."

APPARITIONS

A goat
on the side of a hill
tethered,

a crop
in a pile in the barn
gathered,

a boat
on the tide going out
weathered,

a hawk
in the glide of the wind
hovered,

a chair
in the shine of a room
leathered,

a star
on the rise in the sky
forevered.

SEA HAIKUS

Trickling and tickling
land's dark and lonely edges -
the tricksy blue sea.

Frizzy on the face
and the tangled old man's head -
grey curls of the sea.

Leading to a burst
of light on the whipped up sea -
tracks on trampled sand.

HIGH TIDE

Tide's in full,
up to the prom
it is, one wave
frisky as a striker
jumping to head
the ball from a huge
swinging corner
and the waves
leap, long hair
flipping over
the shore but
no score it's
a draw.

GIANT

Bangs like thunder,
crashes through trees,
great big blunderer,
watch him sneeze!

Taller than steeples,
louder than trains,
eats many peoples,
got small brains.

Carries a club
and one to spare,
makes you blub
to see him glare.

Eye sight blurry
deep set frown,
fat belly hairy,
broken teeth brown.

Out on his owny,
looking for scram,
ever so lonely,
Bam! Bam! Bam!

HALF ASLEEP

Half asleep -

    that's the time for twitches
    and falling into ditches
    and painful little stitches
    and naggy, naggy itches
    and cackling old witches

half asleep
in your bed.

RAIN AGAIN

Rain blows liquid
glass into globes;

plants swelling
tubers of silver;

stitches pearls
onto black dresses

of tarmac down
by the school bins.

ODE TO ROAST CHICKEN

Free of feathers your
pimpled white skin hardly
excites our appetites
but stuffed and buttered
and hidden in the oven's
cave you soon announce
your glory with the sweet
smell of roasting that wafts
throughout the kitchen.

Your best friends, roast
potato, boiled carrot
and broccoli wait in pans
while you rest and naughty
children peel and gobble
your succulent skin.

Gravy, that nectar, poured
from the jug, joins you
and your friends on the plates
and oh the sighs and gasps
that you cause with your
deeply satisfying taste!

For some it is the juicy
dark leg, while others love
those slim white slices
of silky meat from either
side of your breastbone.

'More, more, please more!'
the family cries even though
everyone's already full.

AUTUMN

The sky has poured
chocolate to sweeten
the trees: dark chocolate
and milk chocolate

and the far away hills
are scoops of pistachio
flavoured ice cream.

Very soon the fields
will be turned into cakes,
piped with icing and
later a hand will write
'Happy Christmas'.

OWL CALLS

Owl calls each
a perfect O, capital O
and small o-o-o-o's
threaded on a slack
and moonlit string,
going small and
smaller into dark
bushes of night.

Or shakes his full
moons out onto
the fabric of night
like many dice
or roulette balls.

At first he nudges
a note like the first
push on Newton's
cradle, more dainty
touch than tap.

Later simply he wails
in mournful solitude
beneath encrusted stars
of the winter night sky.

Soon a faraway one
gurgles back and flies,
flattening the rounded
note, muffling the ting
of it, till it is gull's
whinge over dusty
grass and arias are
duets with harsh
howls and squeaks
as dead as prey

when a distant owl
remembers the first
refrains, calls them
to glistening order,
the shining strings
of perfect O's.

SNORING CAT

Our cat snores
I heard her yesterday
curled up in her cosy
basket, snoring away.
Nobody believes me
not a single word.
When they went to
listen, she purred.

FOUR CINQUAINS

Dawn's pink
casts calmness on
the river, mists the trees:
a spell's spoken, a sedative
taken.

Inside
every hello
hangs a little picture
on walls of the future showing
goodbye.

Blackbird
chips away at
the stony cold silence
with his bright and yellow chisel
at dawn.

Mountains
grey and distant
those speechless old giants
shoulder the afternoon sky like
Atlas.

TROUBLES

Do you have trouble
drying between your toes?
Do you have trouble
trying to clear your nose?
Do you have trouble
when your memory goes?
Do you have trouble
when your purple face glows?

WHISTLING MAN

On a chair that isn't there
sits a gold and silver man
whistling like a spring bird.

BLOSSOMS

The hoods of some trees
are white ermine-furred;
others swarm with hairy
white caterpillars;
meanwhile frothy bubbles
wash clean the landscape.

THE GREY SCHOOL

There is a school, The Grey School, every wall
painted grey, floors too, all grey, ceilings grey,
doors grey, all teachers called Mrs Grey or
Miss Grey and Mister Grey the stern headmaster
is battleship grey. He sails the classrooms,
cannons trained on children, colourful kids
who try to understand the grey lessons
as tedious as ash, till they sink in it.

A new teacher came one day, called Miss Brown:
lovely chestnut hair, green eyes, red lipstick
on her mouth and nobody knew where she
came from or who sent her. She arrived at
the start of term with all the new children
and the headmaster reached for his tablets.

Miss Brown was one of those teachers who help
the other teachers. She saw the graphs on
the walls with the black arrows pointing down.
She coloured them green and made them point up.
In secret sessions she taught the teachers
lessons in happy and lessons in joy,
lessons in laughter and lessons in fun,
while Battleship sat at his computer.

Those lessons began to hit their targets:
one grey old teacher grew purple highlights
in her hair and the hands of another
turned green and held a bunch of flowers in
school assembly. One Miss Grey got married
to Mister Scarlet and a fourth one's feet went
yellow with pollen. Finally, the stern
headmaster's face went crimson with anger.
The very next day came decorators
with brushes and cans of colours galore.

CROCODILE

Crocodile slides
like a submarine,
a lumpy, bumpy
submarine, just below
the water-surface
in the river's stream.

Crocodile's mouth
is a yawning trap,
a tooth-terrible trap.
"Come on in,"
he whispers, "into this
friendly gap.....SNAP!"

MISTER HARD
EATING LUNCH

Mister Hard in his tight black t-shirt
opens up his lunchbox.
Young and tough, brim full of fitness,
muscles firm as flint rocks.
Spends his life
in the gym – that's him.

Pulls out a bap stuffed with bacon
opens such a wide gape.
Plunges down his teeth deep and strong
makes a funky ape shape.
Spends his life
in the gym – that's him.

Chomps and chews with manic jaw force
as if he's lifting weights
but Mister Hard isn't pumping iron
it's just the way he eats.
Spends his life
in the gym – that's him.

ON THE MERE

Cranky coot,
with a white
cob on, shrieks
across the pool
and sails his
black boat to
tufty island.

White of swan,
delight of swan
in sunlight, linen
skirt and linen
blouse ruffled,
silky scarf held
with yellow-
black woggle.

Sloucher heron
hangs around on
reedbed corners
secretly smoking,
spitting in gutters,
looking for trouble,
waving a blade,
gobbling a frog.

UNCLE ALLAN THE SHIPBUILDER

Little Uncle Allan with his toothbrush
moustache, squirrel eyes, cheeky grin
came to our house for a bath on Friday
nights, carrying jokes in his mouth
and in his hands bags of sweets
and pocket money coins.

"What's right to say," he'd always
say, laughing like a jackdaw,
"The yolk of an egg is white
or are white?" We'd shout back,
"It's not white, it's YELLOW!"

Like a fisherman then he'd reel out
joke after joke after joke, some rude
until Nan said, "Allan, that's enough.
Think of the children." But we didn't
mind listening to our five foot six uncle,
standing there as straight as a post.
Earlier that very day masked and mighty
he wielded in the shipyard his welding
iron and fired pure blue flame to melt
two great plates into one.

Uncle Allan, the hero, building
ships, great liners that sailed
the seas of the world.

OLIVE AND THE BROCCOLI

mummy's started
      feeding me funny
little things and
i'm not sure i like them
here she comes
          o-oh, o-oh,
what's this floppy stick
with a bush on top
Is it weeds from a pond
flip-flop, flippy-floppy
it goes.......... o-oh
she wants me to put it
in my mouth
         another funny
little thing i don't think
will be tasty
i've got it.....it flopped
i think i'll drop it on
the floor....no mummy
wants me to eat it
         she's pushed it
nearer my mouth
should i put it in...
i don't think so......
ok mummy just to please
you i will.....in it goes....
ooooh mummy i like it
i really do

WINNIE POEMS

1. The New Girl

Winnie's mum and dad
moved the family
from town to a place
of green fields and trees.
New house, new neighbours
and a new school where
she knew nobody.

Miss Robinson smiled,
"This is Winifred,
a new girl, now who
would like to be her
friend and show her round?"
said the kind teacher.
Florence was the first
to put up her hand
and beside her was
an always empty seat,
empty no more.
Florence smiled. Winifred
smiled and sat down
beside her new friend.
The very next day
it was all 'Winnie'
and 'Flo', hide and seek,
tick and skipping and
hopscotch at playtime.

Soon Winnie and Flo
were like twin sisters
sharing everything
going for tea at each
others' houses, loyal
friends for life.

2. The Hen House

Winnie's new house had
a garden with tall
bushes, bright flowers,
a lawn and a henhouse.
No hens lived there so
Winnie's mum said, "This
will make a magic
playhouse for you
and your best friend Flo."
For tables and chairs
Mum begged fruit boxes
from the greengrocer.
She made tablecloths
and curtains from scraps
while Winnie and Flo
swept the floor, and scrubbed
that dirty henhouse
clean as the sky on
a warm summer's day.

They played Red Riding
Hood: Flo as the hunter,
mum as the bad wolf
and Winnie as the
little girl. They played
posh people taking
afternoon tea in
stately homes: "Would
you prefer angel cake
or a buttered scone,
Lady Cavendish?"
said Winnie and "Either
would be spiffing,"
said Flo to Dame Clare
as they sipped their tea.

MAGIC TREE

Magic tree dancing
in the forest, magic tree
with silken wings,
leaves that flutter
yellow and green
from the slim brown
arm of a woodland elf.

OLIVE IN SPRING

Into the park this
clown-faced daffodil
morning, she's walking,
bandy-legged
with her nappy,
arms outstretched
and wrist-dangling,
squealing with joy
at nothing more
than a nod-headed
pigeon or simply
the path and the grass
and the balmy air.
Suddenly she stops.
She points then puts
fingers to lips.
It's profound, it's
a squirrel pouring
itself over the grass,
pausing and twitching
its tail - and satisfied
Olive is off again
and it's ducks, a crow
cawing in a tree,
the sun shining,
blue sky resting,
such marvellous,
significant things.

LITTLE GIRL LOOKS

Little girl looks at her
crooked thumb and says,
I don't like the bent thumb
I want another finger instead.

Little girl looks at her
little paper kite and says,
I can fly, I can draw myself
on this kite and fly.

Little girl looks at her
daddy's spectacles and says,
You have a dish in your eye
with the spoon sticking out.

Little girl looks at four
people walking in pairs and says,
I'll go in between
and make a five dice.

Little girl looks at a
fir cone in her pocket and says,
I have autumn in my hand.

ENDS OF DREAMS

Out with the light and into your bed to
drive a rally car round a mountain bend -
End!
Dream dissolves in the howling of a dog.

Turn over again. Snuggle back down to
fire whistling arrows from a castle wall;
drive a rally car round a mountain bend -
End!
Dream melts away in shouts from the street.

Over on your back, breathing deeply now to
fly a sleek rocket to Venus and Mars;
fire whistling arrows from a castle wall;
drive a rally car round a mountain bend -
End!
Dream falls down with the banging of a door.

Lie flat on your belly, counting sheep to
creep through tunnels to a cave full of gold;
fly a sleek rocket to Venus and Mars;
fire whistling arrows from a castle wall;
drive a rally car round a mountain bend -
End!
Dream evaporates in the headlights' flash.

Hug yourself tight and think of good things to
collect your winnings in the lottery;
creep through tunnels to a cave full of gold;
fly a sleek rocket to Venus and Mars;
fire whistling arrows from a castle wall;
drive a rally car round a mountain bend -
End!
Dream explodes in the scream of the alarm.

STARLING

Guzzlegawk
gormlessly spears soils.

Lawnpirate
rapaciously tosses spoils.

Bullybird
aggressively thrusts beak.

Swaggercrow
bunglingly splays feet.

Roofmocker
raucously murders songs.

Nightflocker
cumulusly sky throngs.

BACKSTROKER

Backstroker!
Can't see where he's going.
Scatter everybody!
Barging rather than flowing.
Scatter everybody!
It's Backstroker.

Backstroker!
Staring at the pebbledash ceiling.
Deepdive everybody!
Doesn't that head have any feeling?
Deepdive everybody!
It's Backstroker.

Backstroker!
Arms like waterwheels whirling.
Changelanes everybody!
Watch out waves are swirling.
Changelanes everybody!
It's Backstroker.

Backstroker!
Feel those hands a-slapping.
Duckdown everybody!
Thick ear if you're caught napping.
Duckdown everybody!
It's Backstroker.

APRIL SONG

Summer days are
coming soon
when sun becomes
a bright balloon,

blossoms dance
on every tree
and birdies sing
'twit, twiddlydee',

flowers sparkle
in the grass,
rabbits spring up
in a flash,

nests soon bulge
with shiny eggs,
kids come home
with dirty legs.

INDEX

Apparitions 17
April Song 41
Autumn 22
Backstroker 40
Blossoms 26
Crocodile 28
Ends of Dreams 38-39
Four Cinquains 25
Giant 19
Grey School, The 27
Half Asleep 20
High Tide 18
Little Girl Looks 37
Magic Tree 35
Mister Hard Eating Lunch 29
Ode to Roast Chicken 21-22
Olive and the Broccoli 32
Olive in Spring 36
On the Mere 30
Owl Calls 23-24
Rain Again 20
Sea Haikus 18
Snoring Cat 24
Starling 39
Tongue-twister's Alphabet 1-14
Troubles 26
Uncle Allan the Shipbuilder 31
Whistling Man 26
WW2 Evacuation Stories 15-16
Winnie Poems 33-35

Dennis Carter lives in Shropshire with his wife Catherine and one very old cat called Peggy. His four children are all grown up and have left home now, three living in London and one in Manchester. For many years Dennis has been going to schools in England and Wales doing poetry and story workshops with children of all ages. He enjoys reading his poems out loud, particularly the funny ones.

Dunstan Carter is a Manchester-based illustrator and writer. He likes drawing funny faces, laughing at sheep and making pies in his kitchen. He also calls Dennis Carter, 'Dad', and likes singing songs about chickens and world peace.

Other poetry collections by Dennis Carter:
Sleeplessness Jungle, 1998
On the Razzle Dazzle, 2001
Shiny Metal Words, 2005
Dance with the Moon, 2007
The Roaring Rainbow, 2010
Shadow on the Run, 2012

Novels for children by Dennis Carter:
Misspellboobiland, 1999
Bringing Home the Dead, 2003
The Sleeping Force, 2009